The Void

Notes On A Few Miscarriages

Rachael Maddux

Vanitas Books

Cover design by Rachael Maddux. Cover image from *Mrs. Robert Shurlock (Henrietta Ann Jane Russell, 1775–1849) and Her Daughter Ann*, by John Russell (1801), from the Metropolitan Museum of Art's Open Access collection.

ISBN: 979-8-9923566-0-1 (paperback), 979-8-9923566-1-8 (ebook)

Contents

Preface

Between March 2018 and July 2021, I got pregnant four times and had four miscarriages, a series of events about which writing was either absolute psychic torture or weirdly so easy. I lost track of the number of drafts I began that seemed promising at first but, like the pregnancies themselves, quickly fizzled out. But when it worked, it worked.

Between February 2020 and July 2022, I published the following essays about my miscarriages through my newsletter, Vanitas. It was important to me to make a public record of these experiences, to kick at the stubborn taboos around pregnancy loss, and to do so mostly without access to narrative resolution—without knowing whether or not I would ever have a child. I hoped that what I wrote would help someone feel less alone, if they'd been through something similar; or, if they hadn't, that it would help them understand what it was like, or at least what it was like for me.

I also wanted to illuminate the gossamer-thin lines between pregnant and not-pregnant, life and not-life, and miscarriage care and abortion care at a time when reproductive rights in the United States were being decimated by lawmakers and judges at every level. Ironically, in June 2022, when the Supreme Court overturned *Roe v. Wade*, I was halfway through my fifth pregnancy; that October, I had a baby girl.

That pregnancy is the subject of the final essay here. In my darkest moments, I resented any miscarriage story with so much as a whiff of a living child, and I resolved to never inflict that pain myself. Now I don't know where to land except in that moment of flummoxed hope. Even then it doesn't feel quite right, doesn't feel whole, but none of these stories do. By their nature, that is the only way to tell them—incomplete.

Starts and Stops
February 2020

The Short Version
I've had three miscarriages.

The Slightly Less Short Version
The first was in May 2018. The second was in January 2019. The third was in May 2019. I was supposed to have a baby in December 2018 and August 2019 and November 2019. But I did not.

Here's Something Cool
The first and the third happened almost exactly one year apart, on either side of Mother's Day weekend!

That Was Supposed To Be Funny
"See, what did I tell you? She's funny," my gynecologist said to the nurse during one of my many follow-up appointments last summer. "Always with these jokes!"

"Ha ha I'd be dead otherwise," I said, and everyone laughed. I'm still not sure how much I was kidding.

Just So We're Clear

I am not currently pregnant. This is not me bundling my past heartbreak in the cozy fleece of happy news. This isn't a footnote. This is the body text. This is the only story I am telling you right now.

But How Am I, Really?

In this moment, right this second, as I'm typing this, I'm actually doing alright. I'm sitting here with my dog, and my husband is about to make a stir fry for dinner. Earlier I put away some laundry. Later, we'll probably watch an episode of *The Young Pope* then go to bed. Maybe, before I fall asleep, I'll read one of the two good books I'm working through right now. Maybe I'll have some ideas about the next draft of my own book and have to hop out of bed and fetch my phone across the room and email to myself. Maybe I will fall asleep easy and wake up feeling good.

That would be nice.

But who knows? Some days I think I'm doing good and then something happens and then I'm not doing good anymore. "It sucks in a pretty pervasive way," I told a friend the other day, and as I wrote that I was like, *Aha! I'm stealing that.* As if somebody else said it.

When I'm not doing good the version of me who could say something like that does seem like another person, though. Sometimes the little gray cloud floats on the horizon. Sometimes it floats directly over my head. Sometimes I'm the cloud.

The Worst Thing About Miscarriage

What I planned to type next was, "is that there's so much bad writing about it!" But that isn't entirely true. I've just spent way too much time on the messageboards.

The actual worst thing is that there are so many potential candidates for Worst Thing that I would have to do it like one of those bullshit awards ceremonies for kids where everyone gets a prize so no one feels left out, like the time at drama camp when I got the Carol Burnett Award For Physical Comedy, which was just those words written in Sharpie on a piece of paper shaped like a blue ribbon.

Actually, in retrospect, that was pretty cool. I just had no idea who she was.

I Just Googled "carol burnett" + miscarriage

Because this is what I do now! Just casually browse the internet for any evidence that any woman whose name crosses my mind might have once slopped around in the same shit bucket as me! The results are not zero but they're all about somebody else: Scarlett O'Hara, a Duggar wife, Meghan McCain.

USA Today: "Meghan McCain felt 'petrified' about revealing miscarriage but decided to 'take the leap'"

I remember reading the *New York Times* op-ed she wrote about her miscarriage and feeling the most disorienting mix of empathy and rage. This was last summer. She and I were both 34, hers happened around the same time as my third, I was in a general mood to deeply relate. But something about it just incensed me. I don't want to ruin my

3

good mood with fact-checking but I believe my rage related to her use of "we"? "We" knew and loved our babies even if we never met them. "We" are no less mothers than women with children in their arms. I don't doubt she felt that sincerely but oh my god the nerve of that first person plural.

Whatever was inside me—they weren't babies. They weren't even fetuses. They were barely embryos. I didn't love them (yet). I didn't know them (yet). They stood me up. They ghosted before our first date. They were strangers to me. I am not a mother of three. I'm not a mother of zero. I am not a mother at all. That's the whole problem here.

Here's Where We Talk About "Heartbeat Bills"

This time last year, the Georgia state legislature was batting around HB481, also known as the Living Infants Fairness and Equality (LIFE) Act, which aimed to make abortion illegal after six weeks, the point at which (supporters claimed) a heartbeat can be detected. Something like this seems to come up every few years down here but it had never been passed before so I didn't expect it would get far this time either. But Brian Kemp was still riding high on his stolen governorship and the bill zipped right through the House and into the Senate.

I knew my own Senator would vote against it but I felt furious and helpless, so I wrote a letter to the members of the Senate Science and Technology Committee—which, if I recall correctly, was comprised of one white woman and a doughy baker's dozen of white men.

Dear Senators,

My name is Rachael Maddux and I'm a resident of Atlanta, represented by Elena Parent in the State House.

I'm writing you today to ask you to please do everything in your power to see that HB481, which would ban abortion after 6 weeks, does not become law in the state of Georgia.

There are so many reasons that this legislature is misguided and deeply harmful to women in Georgia. Many of these were articulated last night by your colleagues in the House, namely Park Cannon and Renitta Shannon. Women have the constitutional right to make their own choices about their bodies and their healthcare, and this bill would absolutely violate that right.

Many women don't know they're pregnant at 6 weeks, and even those who do know that early don't always have necessary access to medical care at that point—or ever. The state of prenatal and maternal healthcare in Georgia is already abysmal, which the effects of this legislation would only compound and be compounded by. And as history has shown, limiting access to abortion doesn't decrease the number of abortions—only the safe ones.

Georgia's maternal mortality rate is already the worst in the nation. If HB481 becomes law, even more women are going to die. Its passage may be a political victory, and perhaps that's all its supporters really care about. But in reality, people are going to suffer. Your constituents are going to suffer. Many are already suffering, and they will suffer more. There will be blood and it will be on your hands.

I'm writing to you today as a woman who has been pregnant twice in the last year. Both pregnancies were wanted and planned for, and both ended in miscarriage. I've always believed that a woman shouldn't have to be pregnant if she doesn't want to be, and my two brief experiences with pregnancy have only increased my resolve. Being pregnant, for a woman, is life-altering and, in too many cases, life-ending. It is a massive undertaking—physically, emotionally, financially, existentially. And it is deeply, essentially personal.

Whatever happens in a pregnancy should be the choice of the woman whose body is growing the child. It is no business of the State of Georgia. Support your citizens, help them thrive, and trust them—especially women —to make their own choices about their own lives and bodies.

Thank you.

Sincerely,

Rachael

Lion, Lamb

That was March 8. On March 22, the Senate passed the bill. On March 26 I found out I was pregnant for the third time.

I Went To The Doctor And The Doctor Said

"I completely understand why you want that ultrasound as soon as possible this time, because of what happened with your other two pregnancies, but really, we don't recommend ultrasounds at six weeks because it's often too early to detect the fetal pole."

"Ha, well, tell that to the great state of Georgia."

"Don't even get me started." I swear she had to crawl under her desk to retrieve her eyeballs, they rolled so hard.

We laughed, at least. At least we laughed.

Now I'm Angry Again

That was also supposed to be a joke. Because I'm always angry!!!

I'm Sorry, Too

I know I shouldn't be but I am. It's hard not to feel responsible when the thing that has gone wrong went wrong inside your own body. It's hard not to feel like apologizing when you're making people all around you so sad, even if you're the saddest of them all. But I am, really. I'm sorry if you don't know me and this is too much to know about a stranger. I'm sorry if you do know me and you wish you'd known about this sooner. I'm sorry if anything like this has happened to you.

I Do Wonder

We have physical comedy, but do we have physical tragedy? What would that be? Is this it?

Garlic

I told myself I was going to sit down and write for a couple hours and see what happened. Now I smell dinner happening in the next room. I'm taking that as a cue to wrap up, otherwise I'll be here all night long or possibly forever.

Here's what I know: I don't know if I'll ever have a baby. (Or what I consider a baby, at least. By Meghan McCain's standards, I should be in the market for a minivan by now. Buckle up, ghosties!!!) But I will always be a person who has had at least three miscarriages. I'm trying to figure out what that means.

This isn't the first time I've written about this. It's just the first time I've written while fully knowing that it will be in the world. There are more rough edges and sharp corners than I'd like, and also more soft bits. Feints and distractions.

As if anyone could tell me I'm doing this wrong.

I don't know how to end this because there's no end, not

yet and maybe not ever. I can always get started and I can never figure out how to stop. The final sentence is always so important to me—I never feel done until I feel good about the last few words. I want them to be magic. I want them to redeem everything. Maybe that's why they never do.

Layovers
September 2021

Nobody should have to be pregnant if they don't want to be pregnant. I have believed this since I was a teenager. I grew up in Tennessee, in what's often called the "most churched city in America," so this was not a belief I came to easily. But I felt very sure of it, once I did, along with a passel of related convictions, among them: either you were pregnant or you weren't, either you wanted to be pregnant or you didn't, abortion was either legal or illegal, either you'd had one or you hadn't. Back then it all seemed very obvious to me, a person who had never had an abortion, who had never even been pregnant, who in fact had never had sex. The right to that choice struck me as absolutely fundamental. And it still does. But I'm less certain than ever about all the other stuff.

Have I had an abortion? My answer is the same as if you'd asked me whether or not I've been to Salt Lake City: "Well, *technically*." I've had a few layovers; I've seen the city from a decreasing then increasing altitude, the mountains, the weird saline expanse; I've shuffled from one terminal to the other, eaten a sad sandwich, half-read a book while eavesdropping — and all of this did happen in the

84122 zip code. So it feels like a lie to say no. But it also feels like a lie to say yes.

I've been pregnant four times and all four of those pregnancies ended on their own. I guess that's a weird way to put it, because most pregnancies "end on their own" when the baby comes out. But I don't have four babies. I don't even have one baby. I've never even been pregnant with a fetus, technically speaking, just an embryo. Four thwarted maybes, four ghosts in the back of my also-nonexistent minivan. (Yeah, that's one more since last year.)

In my medical files, the miscarriages are noted as "spontaneous abortions." I've had nurses apologize for the "abortion" part — "I know that's upsetting to see, so sorry, it's just the technical term!" — but what always strikes me is the "spontaneous." Personally, I like making a plan and sticking to it. But my abortions, hey, they're really living in the moment! Love that for them, YOLO, etc.! At least one of us is having fun!!!

"Ended on their own" is also weird to say about my pregnancies because, actually, none of them all the way did. My miscarriages have all been "missed" miscarriages. Each time, the pregnancy stopped developing at some point early on but declined to notify the rest of my body, punting responsibility to the ultrasound tech at my first or second appointment. And so each time I've required some degree of medical intervention to make it really, truly over.

The first three times, I had a D&C. The fourth time I took a dose of misoprostol, and when that didn't get the job done, I had an MVA. (And that's when I started referring to my uterus as the Hotel California.) I've Googled all of these things many times, and I could Google them all again now, but honestly I don't feel like it. Do it yourself, and you might notice what I always do: that the websites and PDFs in the search results are almost always intended for people having an abortion.

That's because the procedures for having an "elective" abortion and dealing with an incomplete "spontaneous" abortion are functionally the same. A world in which healthcare professionals apologize for the use of standard medical terminology isn't a world in which this information is readily volunteered, so you may or may not know this? But it's true. They are the same. They end pregnancies that are wanted and unwanted and somewhere in between. They bring sorrow and relief and wild ambivalence. They're never entered into lightly, or if they are, who cares? They're essential. They've made my life and many others possible.

I've thought about this so much over the last few years. My own personal reproductive shitshow has played out against a terrifying surge of anti-choice laws across the United States, particularly in the South. In Georgia, where I live, our GOP-choked General Assembly passed HB 481 and our exquisite turd of a governor signed it into law within less than a month in the spring of 2019 — a span of time that wound up comprising most of the brief entirety of my third pregnancy. I was still reeling from number four when the Supreme Court allowed the imminently cruel new Texas law to go into effect on September 1.

Look, here come the caveats: I'm a white lady. I have resources, including good health insurance. If I needed an abortion, legal or otherwise, I feel reasonably certain that I could figure out how to get one. My fear and my anger is largely for all the people who don't have that privilege, or those resources, or that (perhaps illusory!) confidence that they'd figure it out. Everything this great backsliding will take from them — has been taking from them — is the primary tragedy, and why it has to be fought.

But even then I am scared in a profoundly selfish way. I may have more miscarriages in the future. And if a law like the Texas law has by then come to Georgia, as I suspect it will, what then? Will I be sued by a bounty-hunting stranger for attempting to access basic medical care? What would they think if they saw "spontaneous abortion" on the medical file? Will it matter that the baby, or the thing that might have become a baby, is no longer alive, was barely alive to begin with? And if it does matter — why? Why should I or anyone deserve that grace more than anyone else?

Order Status
November 2021

I n early June, I bought a couch. It was one of those direct-to-consumer things where you can pick out every little detail: fabric color (moss green), leg finish (walnut), seat number (three), chaise lounge extension (yes). It was on sale, the afterglow of Memorial Day, but it was backordered, estimated delivery in 10 to 12 weeks. Funny, I thought, how it was the pandemic that made me realize we needed a new couch, one where Joe and the dog and I could all stretch out our legs at the same time, and now the pandemic was mostly over and would certainly be all the way over by the time the couch arrived in 10 to 12 weeks, mid-to-late August.

What would that world be like, the world when our couch would arrive? I wondered if my office would be reopened, if we would be eating inside restaurants without thinking twice, if we would've gone to Maine to make good on the trip we cancelled in May 2020. I wondered if I would be pregnant by then. I did the kind of math that has become more natural to me than algebra ever was and calculated that, if I got pregnant in June, then the pregnancy and the couch would be moving on the same timeline.

If you're unfamiliar with the many bizarre Terms of Use of pregnancy, you may not know that the weeks and days in which pregnantness is generally measured start not when you learn you're pregnant, or the moment the fertilized embryo implants, or the day of ovulation, or any other nebulous point along the way. No, the count starts the first day of your last period, a day that famously indicates that you're not pregnant. So whenever you discover that you're pregnant, some revision is required. You get that positive test and all of a sudden, a number of weeks of your life — two (if you have an "average" cycle") or more — must be retroactively gerrymandered into this weird new territory. I have a sense that this is something most people forget about eventually, as they're drawn deeper into the indignities of pregnancy then ground out the other side with a new baby and a new self to care for. But I fixate on it, maybe because those few non-pregnant weeks feel bigger when they're part of a pregnancy that ends barely after it began (as mine have all been).

Anyway, in early June, when I ordered the couch, I wasn't pregnant. But by mid June I was pregnant and by late June I knew it, so the whole month was annexed. By the time the new couch arrived, allegedly, I would be teetering on the brink of the second trimester.

In July, I spent a lot of time on the old couch. I lay there trying to watch TV, trying to read, trying to not hate food, trying not to worry, then giving up and just falling asleep. Sometimes Joe and the dog sat with me, all of us curled up together, and then I felt sad that I'd ordered a new couch when we'd had so many cozy times on this one, and maybe there wasn't anything wrong it with after all, maybe stretching out our legs was an overrated luxury, maybe I told myself we needed a bigger couch with a chaise lounge extension when really I just wanted something to change after a year of not much change and buying a couch seemed like the easiest thing. Other times I dared to picture myself still pregnant however many months in the future, and sometimes I even dared to imagine us with a baby some months after that, and in those moments a bigger couch seemed actually quite prudent. Then Delta spiked and it seemed not just prudent but necessary because who knew if we would ever be leaving the house again? The office was not reopened. We ate inside one restaurant before retreating to takeout. We once again cancelled the trip to Maine.

And then in late July, eight weeks into the 10 to 12 week couch wait, eight weeks into the pregnancy, I wasn't pregnant anymore. Or I was, but in the inverse of the way in which I'd been pregnant for those two weeks in early June, the ones where I wasn't pregnant until later when I was pregnant. Here I'd been feeling like a pregnant person, eating and worrying and sleeping like a pregnant person, and for weeks the pregnancy, the thing itself, had been acting like nothing. Not living, not growing, only tricking me.

I was very sad but not surprised. All along I'd wondered if I would still be pregnant by the time the couch arrived. Still, it wasn't the bad-news ultrasound that made me realize this wouldn't be happening, or the subsequent weeks of dealing with the miscarriage, but the UPS shipping notification that gave the estimated delivery date of Friday, August 27. I wasn't in the mood to trust it, but sure enough, that afternoon three gigantic boxes appeared outside our house, 12 weeks on the nose.

Except — there were supposed to be four boxes? And there were supposed to be legs and bolts and things to connect the contents of the boxes to themselves and one another. And the Order Status page on the website only said "Shipped!" And customer service wasn't going to answer an email on Friday night. Or Saturday. Or Monday, even. Tuesday, the missing legs and bolts arrived. Tuesday, customer service replied to tell me the final box, the chaise lounge extension, had yet to ship. We assembled what we could. The moss green looked nice. The walnut legs looked nice. The new couch was indeed bigger than our old couch. The dog liked it. It was a good couch. But it wasn't the *whole* couch? I became obsessed with the couch and its incompleteness. I spent much of week 13 refreshing the Order Status page and it only ever said, "Shipped!" Every day I waited for the grind and sigh of the UPS truck. Every day it did not come, or it came and brought something other than what I wanted. Edging into mid-September, week 14, I got an automated email asking me to rate my Customer Service Experience. I typed, "Well, since you asked...!" Blood pounded in my skull, just like, all the time. A week went by (week 15) before they replied to tell me that the the fourth box, the stupid chaise lounge extension, had been lost in transit. An apology was issued. A claim was filed. A replacement was ordered. A partial refund was offered. A partial refund was accepted.

I hate passive voice — I find it irresponsible — but I had three-fourths of a couch, I was not pregnant, I didn't know why, I don't know why, everything mattered, nothing mattered, everything felt lightyears beyond my understanding or control. My marbles were lost.

Then one night, late week 16 or early week 17, I got an email: "Your order arrives tomorrow!" But the order did not arrive tomorrow. Instead came another email: "Your order arrives tomorrow!" The next night: "Your order arrives tomorrow!" The next night: "Your order arrives tomorrow!" The next night: "Your order arrives tomorrow!" The next night: "Your order arrives tomorrow!" The next night: "Your order arrives tomorrow!" The next night: "Your order arrives tomorrow!" The next night: "Your order arrives tomorrow!" The next night: "Your order arrives tomorrow!" The next night: "Your order arrives tomorrow!" The next night: "Your order arrives tomorrow!" The next night: "Your order arrives tomorrow!" All through week 18 and into week 19. "Your order arrives tomorrow!" Every night Joe knew when the email came in because I would theatrically gasp, "Guess what—!" I resigned myself to continuing the bit for the rest of our lives together. Then one night, nothing. The next night: nothing. Nothing. Nothing.

Every single day, I thought about cancelling the order. I thought about the stupid chaise lounge extension in its gigantic box, one box among however many boxes stuffed into the hull of a massive cargo ship, the ship itself one of however many clogging some overburdened port, clogging the water and the air with their idling fumes, killing the birds and the fish, killing us all. I was embarrassed that I ever wanted it, embarrassed that I ordered it, embarrassed that I was obsessed with it, embarrassed that I was so angry. I deserved it and also I didn't deserve this!!! I should have just gone to Rooms-to-Go like my parents would have, bounced my butt on some real-life cushions, stroked some microfiber swatches, and paid actual money for an actual couch that already existed and could be trucked right to my door, all parts and legs present and intact, no drama, no tension, no suspense.

I felt certain that I should cancel the order in the same way I felt, when I learned in late July that I was having another miscarriage, that I was done, absolutely one-thousand-percent done, with wanting to be pregnant and trying to be pregnant and being pregnant and trying to have a baby. Both desires hit me with the same panicked certainty, this feeling of *get me out, get me out, I have to get out.* Flailing, thrashing.

Sometime back in September (week 13?), I read an essay by the writer Danielle Lazarin about the awful limbo of having a book on submission to publishing houses for a very long time. I read it hungrily, breath shallow, eyes wide, in part because that's how I was doing everything, just a little bit desperate all the time, but also because — in addition to the pregnancy and the miscarriage, and the stupid couch, and the stupid Delta variant, and everything else — the memoir I've been writing since 2012 went on submission this spring and... nothing happened. My agent, who is wonderful, tells me there's no cause for alarm, it's just a tight market and a weird time generally, but it's a good book, it will find its home, and I believe that, I believe her. But it's still hard. And so it was somehow both heartening and so, so discouraging to read about Lazarin's book, not her first, being on submission since March 2020, the hope of it selling just dangling there for so long, nothing to say it won't happen, nothing to say it will. "Some days, I get close to asking my agent to pull the book from submission," she wrote, "but there's no good reason to beyond wanting, as everyone else does, to just get to the end already."

I'm pretty sure I gasped when I read that — not theatrically but for real — and every time I've thought of it since then I've just felt like, *UGH UGH UGH SHIT.*

Because she's right. Because for as much as I want my book to be published, and as heartbroken as I am at the prospect that it might not ever be — and for as much as I want to have a kid, and as heartbroken as I am at the prospect that I might not ever — and yeah, for as much as I

18

wanted to sit on this whole entire couch that I ordered what seems like three distinct lifetimes ago, and as maddened as I am by whatever confluence of macroeconomic factors and furniture startup growing pains was preventing that from happening — for as awful as all the worst-case outcomes of these various scenarios once seemed to me, the in-between, the neither-here-nor-there-ness of the waiting time, has come to seem even more odious and unbearable. If I can't get what I want, I want to be the one who says I don't get it, I want to be in charge, I want to take the blame. But mostly I just want to know how it ends.

I know I've done some righteous, or at least rightful, quitting in my life — one disastrous school play, a couple bummer jobs, and I guess a whole religion? — situations that truly were no good for me and that were better off being left behind. But I wonder how often I've cut myself loose just for the sake of doing something, and whether that moment of punctured tension was worth whatever I was giving up.

All this to say, I didn't cancel the couch order. In late October, I emailed customer service "just to check in!" and they said the final part was set to be delivered on November 5. It wound up arriving on November 10, but it arrived. It arrived! Nevermind that it took 22 weeks, nevermind that the time between the first three-fourths arriving and the final one-fourth arriving was longer than my pregnancy this year, nevermind that the presence or absence of any/all part of a couch is a demented thing to fixate on in the midst of the world's ongoing crisis turducken. Nevermind! Because the stupid fucking thing arrived, it finally arrived, it was unpacked, it was assembled, it was made whole.

And I was made whole too! Well, no. I'm still a great tangled mass of unresolved yearning. But the couch is... you know, it's fine. The couch is fine. It feels like it's been in our house for much longer than just a few months, and that's both a testament to the human mind's ability to recover from what feels like unbearable uncertainty as well as a review of the cushion and fabric quality. But it's here. It's here. Joe and the dog and I can all stretch out our legs at the same time, and I guess that's what I wanted, I guess that's enough for now.

A Charm
July 2022

The first time we were going to Maine — May 2020 — it was three nights in a "stunning 1 bdrm apt" in Portland, two nights in a "custom designed tree dwelling" in Georgetown, and three nights in a cottage in Bar Harbor with "a sunny (usually) porch." Why Maine? I don't even remember. The goal was to avoid Mother's Day, the anniversary of two-thirds of my miscarriages up to that point, although it would be Mother's Day in Maine, too, I realized eventually, so I guess the true goal was just to be sad somewhere I'd never been sad before. Despite the volume and frequency of my sadness, many fine locations qualified! But Maine had seafood and beer and crags and trees, and legal weed, and this bagel place our friends really liked, and the L.L.Bean store with the really big boot? And Joe liked the sound of it too. So I booked the rooms, the flights, the rental car. We would obliterate the cursed day with air travel, then spend the week nestling deep into one limbo inside another inside another.

We would, and then we would not. Until then, I'd never canceled a trip before. I was surprised to learn that it's easy, actually—way easier to cancel travel plans than to make them. Get some refunds, eat some fees. On Mother's Day we were nowhere new, but then again neither was hardly anyone else; we FaceTimed our moms then resumed the ninth week of lockdown, a limbo all its own. "Next year," we said, "next year" — and I didn't know what we meant, and I didn't know if I believed it either way.

* * *

The second time we were going to Maine — August 2021 — it was three nights in a Portland apartment "in a vibrant, transitional neighborhood," three in a tiny house in Stonington "with a faint view of the harbor," and a final night back in Portland in something called the "Green Eyes" room at a "one-of-a-kind guest house and social gathering space." We were freshly double-vaxxed and eyeing the summer like famished hounds. The first attempt at Maine had been all about avoidance; the second would be vengeance. Everything that hadn't happened for so long was going to happen again and/or at last. I booked the rooms, the flights, the rental car. We would land the week of our tenth wedding anniversary, peak blueberry season. We don't have any particular passion for blueberries but even that felt like a triumph. And I was pregnant again, just barely. Everything was *just* barely.

It was, and then it was not. The Delta wave rolled in and I had an iffy ultrasound and I felt like shit. I'd canceled the trip before and I knew I could cancel it again and then I did. Refunds, fees. The day before we would've been flying to Portland, another ultrasound, this one definitive. The day we would've been driving to Stonington, a dose of misoprostol. On our anniversary, brain-pulping pain and blood blood blood. "Next year," we said again, "next year" — long past questioning how many limbos a person can safely exist within at the same time.

* * *

The third time we were going to Maine — June 2022 — it was six nights in Portland only at a bed and breakfast that "recently dropped the breakfast." Less schlepping if we made it, less canceling if we didn't, both options appealing because now I was pregnant for the fifth time. Our attempts to visit Maine and our attempts to have a baby had come to seem so cosmically thwarted that I wondered why I wondered if this time would be any different. Of course it would. But of course it wouldn't. What do you call this— equanimity? Ambivalence? Bone-headedness in the face of reproductive trauma and a never-ending global pandemic?

Both outcomes of both scenarios seemed equally possible and equally impossible, and I expected the scales would remain balanced just so, right up until the moment they threw themselves horribly askew once again. This is where I landed, after all these years of trying to make rough peace with the fundamental uncertainty of human existence. If I was ever inclined to believe in a sure thing, I'm not anymore, and I'm mostly grateful for that. But along the way — in an ironic effort to make the uncertain more certain — I forgot that there can be gradients to the unknown, gray zones within gray zones. Maybe it's not wise to feel too sure about too many things in this world, but there's much to be said for letting yourself feel sure *enough.*

All this to say, the moment I realized we were probably actually going to Maine was perhaps the same moment I realized I was probably actually going to have this baby. We were on the plane, on the tarmac at Hartsfield-Jackson, excavating our seatbelts and fussing with our headphones, and I kept thinking, *What's the catch?* We were on the trip and still I was waiting for something to happen and cancel the trip. *What's the catch?* I was asking the same question about my pregnancy, too. I was twenty-one weeks in and everything was going fine. Absolutely unremarkable, absolutely boring, everything I'd ever wanted, more than I ever thought I could hope for. *What's the catch?* For a while it had seemed like a reasonable question. I had every reason to keep my guard up. But there on the plane, flight attendants shutting overhead bins up and down the aisle, I was all of a sudden just so tired. Tired of bracing, tired of tempering, tired of inching along. Something truly wild could still intervene — fuel leak, flock of geese; abruption, malformation — but what were the chances? Not zero. But also not enough to keep holding it all at such a distance.

So I turned to Joe and said, "Oh my god, we're going to Maine!" And he said, "Yeah, we are!" And so we did. We went to fucking MAINE fucking FINALLY and we had a GREAT TIME. I spent so long worrying about whether it would or wouldn't happen, so long dealing with the fallout of the not-happening, that I kind of forgot there was something I wanted on the other side and what might it be like, to be there? Turns out, being there is WONDERFUL. There was indeed seafood and crags and trees. I ate one lobster roll every day, and duck confit poutine, and fried oysters with nuoc cham, and one very large pancake riddled with blueberries and bacon. We scrambled around on rocks that looked like petrified wood, and rocks that looked like ancient whale-backs, and all along the roadsides the wild lupine was blooming and in tidy little yards the dahlias were blooming, and the high was 76 and the mosquitos were asleep or unborn. One morning we got breakfast from the bagel place our friends really liked and drove it up to Boothbay Harbor, where we took a boat ride out to an island to see the hundreds of pairs of puffin and their pufflings salvaged from a population near zero in the 1980s; and guillemot too, and many terns and one seal, and a pod of black dolphins that cut right along our wake. After that the big Bean Boot seemed too obvious, too easy to find, but I made Joe take my picture with it anyway, just like I made him take my picture with the Bigfoot at the International Cryptozoology Museum, its narrow galleries crammed with evidence of things seen and unseen. And there was indeed beer, and there was indeed legal weed, and though I did not partake in either, in deference to the fetus, I was happy as a saint for Joe, who did. "Next time," I said, "next time" — and I don't know if that was a promise or a threat, but for once I like my chances.

Acknowledgments

Thank you to Abby Greenbaum, Hannah Palmer, and Laura McKee for the wisdom.

Thank you to Duvall Osteen for the support.

Thank you to Anna Davis, Mindy Middleton, Dr. Kristen Oates, and Dr. Heather Hipp for the care.

Thank you to the Madduxes, the Landises, and the McCormicks for the love.

And of course Joe, and of course Ramona, for everything.

About the Author

Rachael Maddux is a writer and editor. Her work has appeared in *Oxford American*, *Virginia Quarterly Review*, *The Believer*, and elsewhere. After many years in Atlanta, Georgia, she now lives with her family in Chattanooga, Tennessee, where she grew up.

For more, visit rachaelmaddux.com.